P9-CLO-164

KEY TO THE UNIVERSE, Egg tempera on gesso panel, 24" x 36", 1965. *Joslyn Art Museum, Omaha, NE.* This is my first painting with a mural on a brick wall behind the main figures. The god-like hand in the mural is moving through a battered universe in search of a keyhole (in this case a bricked-up window). The nuns are moving away in ambiguous contemplation.

This book has been published by Ripe Tomato Books with support from Ursuline College. All proceeds from sales of this book will be donated to Ursuline College.

Jacket painting:cover image: LIGHT SPANGLES, Egg tempera on gesso panel,
24" x 28", 2001. *Private collection.*

Project Director: Mary Wasmer
Design: Lou Robinson, Iron Design

Printed in Canada by Friesens Corp. through Four Colour Imports, Louisville, Kentucky.

The typefaces used in this book are 11 pt. Adobe Garamond and 7 pt. Avenir Book.
This book is printed on acid-free paper.
ISBN : 0972129405

Deo, illuminatio mea.

(Lord, enlighten me.)

–Motto of Oxford University

YOUNG NUN, Egg tempera on gesso panel,
17" x 23", 1989. *Private collection, Naples, FL.*

Contents

ROBERT VICKREY'S NUN PAINTINGS

CREATURES OF THE SPIRIT

By Donald Miller

NUNS, Oil on canvas, 17 1/4" x 34", 1949. *Private collection, Naples, FL.* This is my first nun painting. It's vaguely based on something I saw in a photography annual. My cornettes are very inaccurate.

Acknowledgements

LITTLE DID I KNOW where this book would take me. Although I have interviewed many hundreds of artists and have enjoyed Robert Vickrey's painting since high school, I never thought I would meet him until William Meek introduced us in his Naples, Florida, gallery.

Then came interviews with the artist in his studios as well as an excursion with my wife Bette to St. Joseph's Provincial House in Emmitsburg, Maryland. There we were introduced to the habit, the cornette as well as the shrine and museum dedicated to St. Elizabeth Ann Seton. This brought back vivid memories of my young years at Mount Gallitzen Academy, run by Sisters of St. Joseph in Baden, Pennsylvania, where the motto was: *Be a Man.* Who could forget that?

I am indebted to Sister Betty Ann McNeil, D.C., archivist at St. Joseph's Provincial House, for checking and adding many facts and improving my manuscript. I would also like to thank Sister Mary Walter Boyle, D.C., for telling me what it is like to be a Daughter of Charity of St. Vincent de Paul and how she found Robert Vickrey.

My thanks also go to the Rev. Paul Thomas, C.M., archivist, Archdiocese of Baltimore, for background on the Vincentians priests and brothers and The Life and Works of St. Vincent de Paul.

I am also indebted to Bill Meek for his faith in this project and help with photographs and to Mary and Jack Wasmer and their son Martin for making this book possible. I am very grateful also to Robert and Beverly Vickrey for giving generously of their time and recollections. I also salute my wife Bette's enduring patience.

Donald Miller
Bradford Woods, Pennsylvania
July 21, 2001

MORNING LIGHT
Acrylic on paperboard, 28" x 37", 1995
Collection of Florence O'Donnell Wasmer Gallery
Ursuline College

Ursuline College
Learning Center

AS A CATHOLIC higher educational institution, Ursuline College, where this book is being introduced with an exhibition of Robert Vickrey's nun paintings, was founded and is sponsored by the Ursuline Sisters of Cleveland. The presence of religious women and what they represent have been an integral part of Ursuline College since its founding in 1871. Over the years, the Ursuline Sisters, like other orders of religious women, have touched the lives of countless people.

Included among those whose lives have been influenced by religious women are the members of the Wasmer family. It was through the Wasmers' generous gift and spirit of "giving back" that the Florence O'Donnell Wasmer Gallery was established on the campus of Ursuline College. The Wasmer Gallery enhances the quality of students' liberal arts education by providing an avenue for creative and artistic expression. In a similar manner, the gallery functions as a resource to the Cleveland community and beyond in bringing fine art to touch the spirit of audiences.

Artists and their works evoke reactions from their viewers. The work of Robert Vickrey and his paintings on the subject of nuns is the focus of this book. It seems appropriate that the Wasmer Gallery of Ursuline College should be the proud home of the award-winning Vickrey painting, *Morning Light.*

I remember well the Saturday morning in Naples, Florida, when, at the invitation of the Wasmers, six Ursuline Sisters from Cleveland visited the Harmon-Meek Gallery to see the current exhibition. There on the wall in one of the rooms was the Vickrey painting that now hangs in the entrance to the Wasmer Gallery.

To Ursuline College that Vickrey painting represents the gratitude and appreciation of Jack and Mary Wasmer to the Ursuline Sisters. It is my hope that as you read this book and learn more about Robert Vickrey and his fascination with nuns, a deeper sense of spirituality will be touched within you and you will reflect on the meaning of life and service to God.

Although the physical appearance of sisters has changed in recent decades, their impact and influence continue to transform society. May your reading of this book be a contemplative and enlightening experience.

Sister Diana Stano, O.S.U., Ph.D.
President, Ursuline College
Pepper Pike, Ohio
Summer 2002

Robert Vickrey

Robert Vickrey

photo by Donald Miller

Introduction

ROBERT VICKREY is a modern master. Few American artists of the 20th century are so recognized and fewer can claim such an extraordinary degree of popularity. The universal appeal of Vickrey's work is surely derived from its accessibility on one level and yet its mystery on another.

Art since World War II has, with few exceptions, been characterized by a downplay in the artist's mastery of the medium. This art has not been about skill nor has it paid tribute to the triumph of past achievement. It has jettisoned craft in favor of clever innovation. Where Robert Vickrey has parted company with most of his contemporaries is that he not only values technical accomplishment but has also presented us with a level of achievement that challenges the most celebrated painting masters of all time. The post-war era has, frankly, not known a greater technician nor does it possess a more convincing conveyor of the narrative.

What Vickrey says and how he says it are clearly without peer. Robert Vickrey has virtually revived egg tempera as a medium (after 1950) and has redefined its capabilities. This in itself is a most significant contribution. With flawless execution and a profound understanding of the limitations and possibilities of this ancient process, he has given new life to the art of painting. But because one is so easily seduced by the brilliance of his brush, it is easy not to give appropriate credit to the brilliance of his mind. He surely recognizes that technical facility is but a component of artistic achievement.

Robert Vickrey's painting, as in all lasting art, is dependent upon its ability to grab, hold and ultimately affect us intellectually and emotionally. The nun theme has been to Vickrey what Mont Ste. Victoire was to Cezanne or the saltimbanque to Picasso. Intrinsically fascinating, the nun's image carries with it centuries of spiritual as well as historical association. (Interestingly, the traditional habit and clothing designs were born in the great period of faith—the Middle Ages—as was the historical beginning of egg tempera painting.) Robert Vickrey exploits the anachronistic personage of the classically attired sister. His painting magnifies her mystique while celebrating the visual and conceptual wonder of her attire—historically intended of course to hide individuality and female beauty rather than extol it.

In a sense the shroud is in itself enshrouded, and it is precisely the intellectual curiosity and richness of this subject that have drawn Vickrey to them again and again. Each confrontation with the theme seems to bring forth magic. And each work leads us to the realization that Robert Vickrey's genius may be that he understands fully that art exists to help unravel the great mystery of man's mind, heart and soul. Art that has endured reaches into the unknown to bring forth light. It was Picasso who said that art ultimately leads us to the truth. Vickrey's art is a confirmation of this thought, and the path to truth he has chosen is one filled with extraordinary beauty.

Louis A. Zona
Director, The Butler Institute Of American Art
Youngstown, Ohio
September 2001

Creatures *of the* Spirit

CHAPTER ONE

Chapter 1: *Creatures of the Spirit*

THIS IS THE TALE of an artistic obsession that has lasted more than fifty years. The wide popularity of Robert Vickrey's nun paintings both baffle and please their creator.

Vickrey responds spontaneously to the images surrounding him. He, like many artists, does not think of himself as exemplar of any particular style, preferring the term "lyrical realism" to explain what interests him most as a painter.

Except for his seventy-eight TIME cover paintings done between 1957 and 1968, the artist has never been content simply to record what is in front of him. Instead, stimulated by thoughts not easily committed to paint, he first weighs his ideas for their visual possibilities and then portrays a personal world of quiet moods and haunting subject matter.

Vickrey's themes arise from everyday reality and what he views as life's inherent mysteries. He often connects his human subjects with carefully delineated locations. His scenes may be as normal as school playgrounds, murals on brick walls, or children and bicycles on city streets. But even here a sense of aloneness dominates each work. The artist has noted how a childrens' playground resembles a prison with its rules and confinements. His scenes may also offer exotic European or tropical locales, and for years he has delighted in borrowing from the masters with his paintings of imaginary murals.

But no images have dominated his painting or his life more than those of nuns. Vickrey's interest more particularly lies with the Daughters of Charity of St. Vincent de Paul, who refer to themselves as sisters and were the first religious women in Europe to work outside the cloister. Vickrey has painted more than four hundred works depicting these sisters with no end in sight. The white linen head coverings they once wore. called cornettes, enthrall him.

While Vickrey was a student at the Yale School of Fine Arts in 1948, he thumbed through a photography annual. A picture of two Roman Catholic sisters, Daughters of Charity of St. Vincent de Paul, suddenly filled his

Previous page: PARIS '58, Egg tempera on gesso panel, 36" x 48", 1958. *Jane Voorhees Zimmerli Art Museum at Rutgers, The State University of New Jersey, Newark, NJ.*

LABYRINTH, Casein on panel, 32″ x 48″, 1951. *Whitney Museum of American Art. Julia Force purchase.* This is my second nun painting. It was done in the corner of my three-year-old son's nursery and depicts a world of decaying movie posters and distortion mirrors. I was amazed when the Whitney showed it and then bought it.

mind with visual possibilities. He learned that the order was founded by Saints Vincent de Paul and Louise de Marillac in Paris, France, in 1633. With his first painting of one of these sisters, Vickrey began a passion that today makes up the largest body of his work.

His paintings have found a steady market and do not remain on gallery walls long. Although the artist has created many other subjects, the nuns are his favorites. His paintings offer an extraordinary range of interpretations and seem like endless variations on a theme. The paintings might be collected in six broad categories. There are the early paintings in which

Vickrey learned over time to capture the Daughters' habits accurately after many variations. The artist also combines nuns in a meditative mood with patterns or shadows. There are also many works where nuns are shown against brick walls, often depicting witty scenes from art history. Some portray nuns' reflections in windows, often showing shimmering light effects. There are also paintings of nuns in natural landscapes and sometimes in fantasies.

The paintings often suggest the sisters and their cornettes as symbols of purity in a less than pure world. Vickrey sees his work as one place he can challenge this state of affairs. The artist has told Professor Philip Eliasoph, director of the Thomas J. Walsh Art Gallery, Fairfield University, Fairfield, Connecticut:

"In our polluted and toxic environment, the nuns and their attire represent the remnants of an immaculate chastity—they are just too fragile and beautiful to exist in this decaying world. That's why I often contrast a nun with a symbol of a collapsing civilization." Yet Vickrey is not a pessimist; he is an artist always seeking the meaning of life and a fuller meaning of God.

The Daughters of Charity, in their calling as given to God for the service of poor persons, minister in the midst of society's harsher elements. They live communally yet are alone within their own sisterhoods, directing their prayers and services to God, and ever asking for His loving helpfulness to the human family. Vickrey sees his nun paintings as contemplative rather than religious, but their spirituality is evident. The sisters in them often seem to be searching for something, or on their way to somewhere, but the destination is left uncertain.

As with most creative endeavors, Vickrey's painting life has been a solitary pursuit, one he seemed destined to lead. Although he has lived a good life with two happy marriages, is the father of four children and the grandfather of five, he has always worked alone while searching for life's answers. With perhaps the radio playing, or the sound of television or books on tape, he paints without further distraction in two nearly windowless studios. One is on Cape Cod and the other in Naples, Florida. In both he likes natural skylit illumination but may work into the night under artificial light. Customarily, he surrounds himself with several unfinished paintings, some of which he may have begun years before.

In the quiet town of Orleans, Massachusetts, Vickrey's shingled studio stretches inconspicuously under tall pine trees not far from the road. Once a contractor's shop and later used to store boats, it resembles a large garage. It contains a sizable painting space with easels, tables, bookcases, magazines and storage area.

Down the driveway from the studio, past the tennis court, is the artist's cozy ranch house, also shingled in New England style. Rear window walls off the living and dining rooms look through shrubbery to Crystal Lake. Sparkling in the sunshine, the lake drew him to this peaceful place from Fairfield, Connecticut, before which he had lived in New York City, where he was born on August 20, 1926.

Vickrey once built a dock on Crystal Lake. It was soon usurped by depositing ducks, Canada geese and sea-gulls, he recounted in his 1987 collection of personal anecdotes, *The Affable Curmudgeon.* Seeking relief, he placed a female dummy in Victorian bonnet and long dress he had found at a shop in town to frighten them. Vandals began filching the dummy's clothing piece by piece til it was nude. The artist began seating the dummy in a chair on the deck, then a lounge. Later, his son Sean hung it from a tree. Then a hurricane whisked her away. The next summer, rumors circulated in Orleans that a woman had been murdered and her nude body was stuck under water in the lake. Of course it was the errant dummy. This story fits the artist's wry sense of humor.

At his winter studio in Naples, Florida, Vickrey paints in half a small stucco house he owns a mile from the Gulf of Mexico. He paints here in Spartan bareness but lives with his wife Beverly on the beach in a condo-minium tower.

Vickrey's earliest years were spent near Reno, Nevada, when, after his parents divorced, he grew up on the Lazy-Me Ranch. Vickrey lived there with his mother, stepfather and half-brother, Caleb Van Heusen Whitbeck, Jr. The boys had a happy early childhood. Vickrey attended a one-room schoolhouse with a single teacher for all eight grades and was allowed to draw and paint most of the day. The first subject he drew was the Lazy-Me cattle brand.

Vickrey's mother died in 1936. Then nine and a half years old, the boy returned to New York City to live with his father, Claude Vickrey, who had resigned from the Navy and was a partner in an insurance agency.

Although puzzled by his son's interest in art, the senior Vickrey never discouraged him, eventually sending him to the Harvey School, in Hawthorne, a boarding school near White Plains, New York. Vickrey then attended Pomfret School, in Pomfret, Connecticut, where he remained through his high school years.

At Harvey, after classes, Vickrey would climb through a window to work alone in the art room, although he was expected to be on the playing field until 5 p.m. He painted to his heart's content in decadent warmth. In those days it was considered unhealthy for growing boys to be indoors before 5 p.m. Yet he was still an athlete and loved soccer. At Pomfret, still wanting to be in the art room after classes, he had to attend football games. At first he checked in at the game, then returned at halftime—he knew when by watching through the art room window—then he would go back to painting. His ruse was discovered. He was not interested in football but had

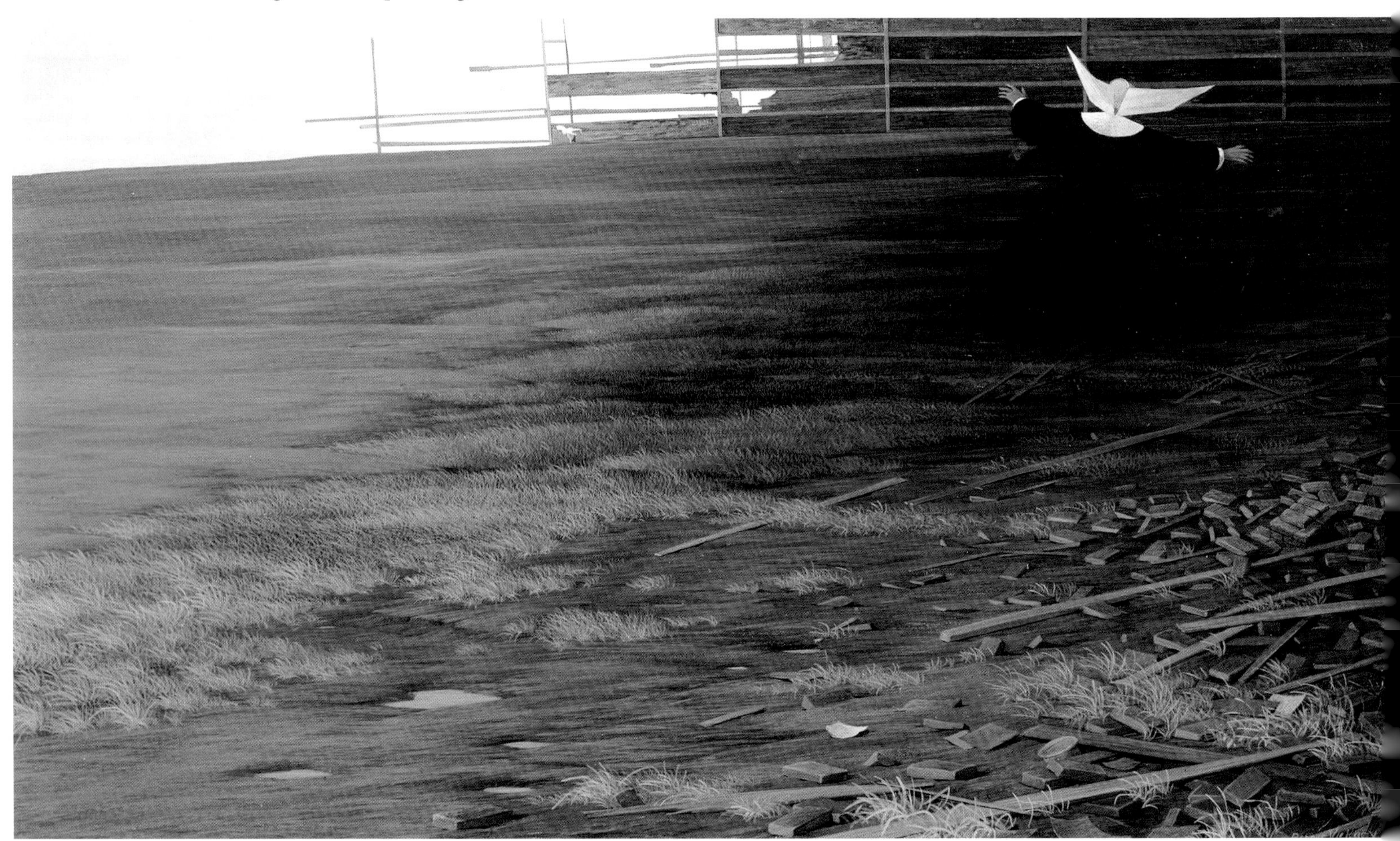

FRIGHT, Egg tempera on gesso panel, 24" x 36", *Collection of Mr. & Mrs. Ronald H. Bell, Naples, FL.* I often paint several versions of a picture. This one is similar to FEAR (page 14) and shows a nun fleeing from an unknown menace. The structure in the background is part of a burnt-down roller coaster at Coney Island.

to report to a monitor and be present at games and practice instead of being permitted to paint. Many years after leaving, The Pomfret School, to the artist's amusement, once named him alumnus of the year.

Although entered at Harvard University, Vickrey joined the United States Navy. It sent him to Wesleyan University in Middletown, Connecticut, where he stayed two years.

All these early events had a role in the artist's psychological development; perhaps none more than his wanting to draw and paint while classmates played. But there are other, more pronounced reasons for his professional solitude.

Changes in the art world were already well underway when Vickrey was a student. The rise of abstraction that would overshadow all forms of realism set him and many other artists adrift from the 1950's nonobjective American art mainstream—as well as the styles that would follow it. Today, Vickrey believes Pop Art, in denying any subjective meaning in its expression, was more hurtful to lyrical realism than abstract expressionism ever was. But he never wavered from his painting style, that he describes as lyrical realism.

While still young, Vickrey knew he had considerable artistic ability. But he soon learned the art world's downplaying representational art would, for the most part, deny him serious critical attention. He enjoys some abstract expressionist art, particularly that of the 1950s, but it is evident it was not for him—especially when he notes collectors liken his unfinished paintings to abstractions. Except when he has chosen to use other than totally realistic means—a factor he and other realists learned from abstraction—the difference between Vickrey's work and abstraction is clear.

Today, Vickrey takes great satisfaction in knowing a large part of the public loves his art with one hundred and twenty-five of his paintings currently owned by museums. That includes forty-eight of his cover portraits for TIME that were then given by Time Inc. to the Smithsonian Institution's National Portrait Gallery. Throughout his career Vickrey has both endured the stress of being outside of critical recognition for most of his life and enjoyed prospering beyond his wildest dreams.

In the 1960's, he earned as much as Yankee hitter Mickey Mantle. At the Harmon-Meek Gallery in Naples, where he has had solo exhibitions annually since 1981, he recently sold twenty-nine paintings in nine days for $400,000. He laughs when a New York art dealer suggests to him that his work doesn't sell, or when an old art acquaintance says, "I thought you were dead!" But it hurts too—even when he knows the vagaries of contemporary art prejudices among museum curators and critics. Where did Vickrey's artistic ideas come from?

The Cold War's global pall is believed to have accelerated the post-World War II era's "Age of Anxiety" that English poet W.H. Auden named. Its mood paralleled Vickrey's personal unease. He was obsessed with life's dark side and pictured it. Until the Soviet Union's 1989 collapse, nuclear annihilation was present as a possibility. Although some American artists made Cold War tensions part of their work, Vickrey gave this aspect of his work a broader meaning. "Almost all artists are trying to reflect what's wrong with the world," he said.

Vickrey's unease found its way into many of his early paintings. The first nun paintings came from an unspecified malaise reflecting a widespread feeling of social helplessness in America. Post-war changes and lemming-like modernity appeared to push aside older, more trusted values. Vickrey eventually would replace these dark paintings with genre figures, often his own children, seen in quiet actions or contemplation—but still possessing an undefined moodiness.

These works make up a broad group and include all of the nun paintings. The artist agreed with his country's feelings of political rupture and discontent. Vickrey saw life's frequent inequities take form in art experts' downplaying his kind of realism. He never let this prejudice overshadow his personal attitudes and sense of fair-mindedness, but he is always conscious of it.

In the post-war years, European Surrealism, with its individualized dream states, also influenced American artists, including Vickrey. They kept to their own subjects and were often called Magic Realists, since no other labels seemed applicable. The term was meant to imply personal imagery and alienation. Both subjects were outside traditional Realism or Social Realism that had galvanized American artists between the world wars. The term Magic Realism became known in the United States with the Museum of Modern Art's 1943 exhibition *American Realists and Magic Realists.* It portrayed disquieting, fantastic or surreal ideas in sharply focused style.

Under this catchall label came such disparate talents as: Peter Blume, Paul Cadmus, Phillip Evergood, Jared French, Henry Koerner, Jack Levine, Charles Rain, Priscilla Roberts, George Tooker, John Wilde, Andrew Wyeth—and Vickrey, who has always rejected the term. Magic Realism was first used to describe French Surrealist Pierre Roy, who was influenced by Giorgio de Chirico and Germans Georg Schrimpf and Alexander Kanoldt in the post-World War I era.

Schrimpf and Kanoldt were also associated with the German Neue Sachlichheit (New Objectivity). This was not a movement, but a way of commenting on everyday reality that deliberately avoided the German Expressionists' obsession with subjectivity. If he has to be called something, Vickrey prefers to be known as a Lyrical Realist. He was pleased with *Robert Vickrey—Lyrical Realist,* the title of a beautiful twenty-eight-minute PBS profile. Vickrey was impressed with how well his images were caught on film, a medium in which he has long been interested.

He once wrote freelance articles for *The Cape Codder* and film reviews for *The Orleans Oracle.* Earlier he wrote and directed seven short art films. They were mostly starkly black, white and grainy, but some garnered positive reviews and prizes. One, to his great pleasure, ran for five weeks in a New York City theater. Another Vickrey film, *The Texture of Decay,* was made at the same time as his painting with the same title. In both he depicted a world gone berserk and used Coney Island's burned-out Luna Park as a background. The movie's climax is the world's cataclysmic end. After dispatching mankind, Vickrey resumed painting and has remained dedicated to it.

In *The Affable Curmudgeon*, Vickrey wrote that he believes we all inhabit a world similar to the one Alfred Hitchcock depicted in his movies. There, Vickrey states, "Something strange and unnerving is always going on

NUN AND POSTERS, egg tempera on gesso panel, 14" x 28", circa 1953. *Private collection.*

just beneath the placid surface of our lives." Hitchcock's sources were post-World War I German and Russian motion pictures filled with psychological distortions of reality.

In 1981, Vickrey told an interviewer that he had "a gloomy view of life, which always comes out in the paintings." But the interviewer, Jeffrey Wechsler, now senior curator of The Jane Vorhees Zimmerli Art Museum, Rutgers University, found any such side to Vickrey's temperament rarely visible in his work by that time. There is even less now.

Today, the artist's sunny home environments, as well as the European locations he has photographed on summer trips, fill his paintings—or they may be completely fictitious. Vickrey is adept at using masks and screens that he cuts himself to create the illusion of leaves and other shadows often seen in his paintings. Helping his present mood is a happy second marriage to Beverly Rumage Vickrey, whom he had first dated in college before meeting his late wife Marjorie.

As a young man, Pablo Picasso once painted a Daughter of Charity of St. Vincent de Paul ministering to a dying man, Vickrey recalled. And like Andrew Wyeth, who in 1992 painted a number of watercolor portraits of an elderly Daughter of Charity wearing a cornette, Vickrey has a devoted following of fans and collectors.

After graduating in 1947 from Yale University with a bachelor of arts degree, Vickrey enrolled at the Art Students League of New York. There he studied with American realist Reginald Marsh (1898-1954) and Marsh's teacher Kenneth Hayes Miller (1876-1952).

Vickrey recalls humorously Marsh's insisting on "rounder forms" from his students. These dominated Marsh's own bustling scenes of Coney Island and Manhattan. But Miller insisted on "flatter forms," influenced by the Italian Renaissance. As usual, Vickrey found his own way between these polarities. He loved the League but hated having to pack up his materials after two or three hours of class, because it destroyed his concentration.

So he returned to the Yale School of Fine Arts to earn a bachelor of fine arts degree. He was permitted to complete five years' work in two.

Vickrey's traditional professor had revived teaching the Renaissance painting technique of egg tempera. This was an important discovery for him. At first he did not like the tedious approach. He soon became enthralled and modernized it, making it his favorite medium. Today he is recognized as one of the medium's American masters.

As a Yale student, it was impossible for him to miss the growing impact of abstract thought everywhere. Although Vickrey understood abstraction's theories, he was not comfortable with them. Yet, like realist contemporaries Paul Cadmus, Peter Blume and others, he easily adapted some of abstraction's simplified approaches to his own work. Vickrey's scenes are never a literal reality, but highly edited versions of it. He deliberately leaves out unimportant details to reinforce and intensify others.

But abstract painting, he could see, was forcing realism from the New York galleries. It would soon arrive at Yale, which was trying to shake off traditional techniques.

As he left, an academic coup toppled the realist professors. Their scourge was Josef Albers (1888-1976), German geometric abstractionist. He drove out Yale's traditionalists by making their courses elective. Albers had studied and taught at the Bauhaus, the advanced German school of design the Nazis forced to close. Albers immigrated to the United States in 1933, and after many years at Black Mountain College—a progressive environment in North Carolina—joined Yale in 1950 as a visiting instructor. He would soon become head of the Yale School of Fine Arts.

Albers was pursuing his decades-long painting series *Homage to the Square.* His simple arrangements of flat concentric color fields influenced Op Art painters and Minimalists in the 1970's–1980's. Albers was so fixed on abstraction, Vickrey remembers, he told students in his heavy accent, "Mood is a schvindle (swindle). If you don't do it my way, I suggest you commit suicide." Pursuing realism, Vickrey looked up from his easel one day to see Albers peering at him at close range. "Paint abstract!" Albers ordered and would eventually banish egg tempera in his school.

At Yale, art students were assigned one of many work booths in a large room. Albers once called students together there—to observe the booth a usually absent student had arranged with an empty easel and table. "Albers got down on his knees, crossed himself and said of the bare arrangement, 'This is the greatest work this school has produced!' It was not hard to see why he thought that," Vickrey said. "Everything in the booth was empty and square."

Albers was also unhelpful to another student. Robert Rauschenberg, who studied with Albers at Black Mountain College, recently told this writer, "I could do nothing to please him. His education was by humiliation."

Vickrey, of Scottish and Irish descent, has always been a quiet maverick, doing exactly what he has wanted with his life. He was pleased to leave Yale and return to New York. With a small inheritance from his mother, Vickrey and his new wife Marjorie took a one-room fourth floor walk-up apartment on Jane Street in Greenwich Village.

Soon, following some painting sales, the couple moved to a two-room apartment, where the artist took less space for a studio than the crib of Scott, the Vickreys' first child. There would be three more children: Nicole, Carri and Sean.

Those paintings of the 1950's-60's make up a large part of Vickrey's seemingly timeless images of beautiful youths in pensive, usually solo activities. They have also been among his most popular subjects. In Orleans in September 2000, Sean Vickrey remembered, "Dad's getting me to sit down and pose was a lot of work for him in those days."

What attracted Vickrey to the Daughters of Charity? To him, these gentle women in their dark blue habits and white cornettes were, pictorially, like otherworldly beings. They blended instantly with the artist's romantic ideas of the unusual and what he knew of everyday life's unexpected experiences. Producing paintings on this theme became a delightful experience. Vickrey saw that, despite what abstraction had come to mean to him, the sisters' head coverings were, first and foremost, splendid abstract forms. These winged appendages have intrigued his mind and eye more than anything else in his paintings.

"Everyone is searching for some higher meaning and questioning of life," he has said. "But what I'm trying to do is explore some of these enigmas."

Vickrey, born into an Episcopalian family, but not a religious man, saw these beautifully yet almost archaically garbed women as pristine holdovers from a long-ago past. In the aftermath of Vatican Council II reforms, their community officially gave up the habit and the cornette, impractical in a world of automobiles and airplanes, in 1964. Daughters, when accommodating themselves in a Volkswagen, had used clips to pin back their "wings."

Yet this religious costume continues to strike a chord in Vickrey's imagination. He paints the Daughters of Charity with great regularity, often from imagination, and in naming paintings has moved backward and forward in the alphabet several times.

For Vickrey, the stiff outstretched cornettes seem to defy the modern world's conformism. Originally, without knowing anything about the ways of the Daughters or the actual design of their clothing, Vickrey began

FEAR, Egg tempera on gesso panel, 24" x 36", 1954. *Collection of the Smithsonian American Art Museum, gift of Sara Roby Foundation.*

placing them in his paintings. Today he is somewhat embarrassed by his inaccurate details.

He gained knowledge of the Daughters and made friendships with several of them. The name of his second nun painting is *Labyrinth*. In it, a sister in a largely imaginary habit is seen from the back with her face distorted in a mirrored wall that zigzags as though in a dark fun house. At left are poster images from the movie *Mighty Joe Young* (RKO, 1949) that Vickrey saw at Coney Island's long-razed Luna Park. The labyrinth reflects how Vickrey felt at the time, working in a small bedroom where his son's crib took more space than he did.

The irony of this painting is that a figure already unusual becomes extraordinary in a reflection, the first of many Vickrey works dealing with such images. The sister's face is a version of his, seen in a fun house's distorting mirror. In 1951, the artist exhibited *Labyrinth* in the Annual Exhibition, now Biennial, of the Whitney Museum of American Art, which purchased it. At age twenty-four, perhaps the youngest artist chosen up to then for this honor, Vickrey was amazed to be selected and astounded to learn the museum had bought his entry.

Vickrey paintings appeared in Whitney exhibitions from 1951 to 1958 and again in 1963—nine in all—although always in a small gallery, indicating the waning importance of realism at the museum. For three years he exhibited there twice a year, usually chosen by then director Lloyd Goodrich. "Goodrich had an effect on my life. As a result of the Whitney selection, I was invited to many other important exhibitions."

The Whitney established Vickrey's importance as an artist. He had arrived and would remain, even though the Whitney's curators would move to later styles. It now honors American contemporary artists and those from the past. Vickrey, whose *Labyrinth* is still in the collection, has weathered art's vicissitudes. He is a prize-winning member of the American Watercolor Society, Audubon Artists and the National Academy of Design. He has thrived with and without official sanctions.

THE NUN,Egg tempera on gesso panel, 20″ x 34″, 1955. *Collection of Marcia & Harry Thalhimer.*

THE CONVERSATION, Oil on masonite, 26" x 46", circa 1955.
Munson-Williams-Proctor Institute, Utica, NY.

STUDY FOR NUN WITH POSTERS, Oil on canvas mounted to masonite, 48" x 72", 1957-92. *Collection of Dr. & Mrs. Robert Springborn, Naples, FL.*

NUN #4, Egg tempera on gesso panel, 16" x 24", 1957.
Collection of Peter L. Pappas

WINTER WALK, Watercolor, 26″ x 39 3/4″, 1960, *Collection Sheldon Swope Art Museum, Terre Haute, IN.*

NUN AND POSTERS, Egg tempera on gesso panel, 24" x 36", 1960. *Private collection, Winnetka, IL.*

THE WALL, Egg tempera on gesso panel, 17 1/2" x 12 1/2", 1961. *The New Britain Museum of American Art, New Britain, CT.*

SISTER OF CHARITY, Egg tempera on gesso panel, 23" x 27", 1965. *Collection of Mr. & Mrs. Russell Fleischman, Naples, FL.*

NUN AND THE ARCH, Egg tempera on gesso panel, 24 1/4" x 17 1/4", 1964. *Virginia Museum of Fine Arts, Richmond, VA.*

SHADOWS AND WINGS, Egg tempera on gesso panel, approx 9" x 12", circa 1969. *Private collection.*

NUMBER 54, Egg tempera on gesso panel, 24" x 36", 1970.
Private collection, Naples, FL.

LONG SHADOW, Egg tempera
on gesso panel, 24" x 18", 1970.
Private collection, Indianapolis, IN.

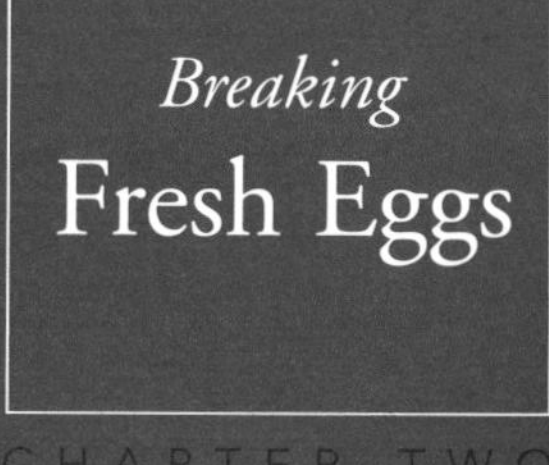

Breaking Fresh Eggs

CHAPTER TWO

Chapter 2: *Breaking Fresh Eggs*

AN UNDERSTANDING OF ROBERT VICKREY'S nun paintings would not be possible without considering egg tempera. In this painting method, the artist cracks a fresh egg and adds the yolk to what is basically opaque pigment. Albumin is gently removed from the exterior of the yolk sac. Vickrey rolls the yolk around on a Kleenex to dry it. He buys powdered pigment in two-pound bags.

Vickrey mixes the pigment and distilled water into a colored paste and pours that for immediate use into a smaller plastic container. To trap impurities, he strains the fatty yolk through cheesecloth. He adds only a small portion of yolk to the pigment before placing it on a paper palette. He keeps the rest of the paste, without yolk, for later use. "You can keep egg yolk overnight but it soon gets moldy," Vickrey said. "It grows a hairy fuzz in the refrigerator—which is why I always use fresh yolks."

Vickrey applies his yolk-paste mixture to an untempered Masonite board prepared for him with gesso on both sides to prevent warping. He does a freehand drawing of the composition directly on the board, then paints with long brushes holding a fine point of red sable hairs. The stiff board keeps the tough but brittle paint from cracking or chipping. An ideal board has a smooth, porous surface and sufficient tooth to hold paint. Although dry to the touch in minutes, a painting needs a year to dry completely. It is then varnished. The artist has more than once found mice and insects have nibbled on unvarnished paintings.

This careful preparation could exasperate oil painters accustomed to buying primed, stretched canvases and ready-to-go pigment in tubes. But each batch of egg tempera must be made with fresh eggs or the mixture will not behave as desired. Pigments may be stored in airtight jars, but if not used within a reasonable time, they harden and become useless. Because egg tempera looks best when built up in several thin coats, it does not cover surfaces as easily or quickly as oils. But then, the effect of the medium's flat but glowing surface is different from oil paint and its somewhat rubbery impasto.

Previous page: THE SHADOW AND THE LINE, Egg tempera on gesso panel, 14" x 21 1/2", 1964. *Indianapolis Museum of Art: Indianapolis, IN, James E. Roberts Fund.*

PATTERNS OF BLUE & WHITE, Egg tempera on gesso panel, 8" x 10", 1970. *Private collection.*

Egg tempera has not just been Vickrey's medium for most of his nun paintings, but his other subjects as well. His approach to it also helps to explain his deliberate mind set. He seldom debates how he is going to paint, but will ponder what he will paint for long periods, even years.

When Vickrey was at the Yale Art School, all students were required to study egg tempera painting. Impatient with procedural dictates handed down from the Italian Renaissance, he has always favored the quicker methods he developed.

Egg tempera was a lost art until 1884, when *Il Libro dell'Arte* (The Craftman's Handbook) by Florentine painter Cennino Cennini (c. 1370-1440), probably written around 1400, was translated into English. None of Cennini's paintings survive, so he is best known for his book—the most important source of art practices of the medieval and Renaissance periods. It describes how followers of Giotto di Bondone (1267-1337) used egg tempera. The Florentine Giotto revolutionized artistic expression by including more naturalism in his compositions.

Vickrey wrote in his 1973 book, *New Techniques in Egg Tempera:*

"Giotto's immediate predecessors vacillated between pallid imitation of his method and the traditional medieval style, with the latter usually winning. So naturalism, which emphasized forms and figures placed in deep space and natural light, took a back seat in Cennini's book. He stressed instead the techniques used by medievalists who constructed form out of purely formal elements—line, light and dark and flat color."

Cennini required at least three drawings before beginning a painting. As though written in stone, his methods were being taught at Yale five hundred years later. "Every time I asked why I had to perform a 'required' step,'" Vickrey wrote, "I was told, in effect, 'Cennini said so.'"

In devising a new methodology, Vickrey quickly increased his painting speed and brought egg tempera into his everyday use. He could paint a TIME cover in a day to meet occasional tight magazine deadlines. He always bought eggs on location rather than toting them to an assignment. Several aspects of the medium still excite him today.

He learned it was not true a painting's composition must be planned in advance down to the last brushstroke and then executed exactly, because supposedly the quick-drying medium would not allow anything else. "That's nonsense. Egg tempera painting is the easiest of all to change or improve. I found by capitalizing on the characteristics of the medium I could expedite my work and at the same time improve its quality." If Vickrey doesn't like a drawing on a panel, he can paint it out and start sketching again in a short time. Because of this, over a long career he has few drawings on paper.

He found that egg tempera does not force an artist to avoid perspective or naturalistic effects, nor does it limit him to small paintings. Botticelli painted such large Renaissance masterpieces as *Allegory of Spring* with its flower-spouting goddess and *The Birth of Venus* in egg tempera. In our era, Andrew Wyeth paints landscapes in the medium.

Egg tempera offers many textural effects. Vickrey loves to create graininess, the defects and rough surfaces of rock, brick and concrete. He can dab or spatter (he likes the word "splatter"), paint and then build up glazes for the exact surface he wants. He also achieves effects by scraping or sanding the paint.

Egg tempera's luminosity is unique. Yolk emulsion enhances pigments' brilliance, creating what the artist calls a shimmering, glowing quality accentuating jewel-like tones. Yet its matte, flat-looking surface tends to heighten composition's linearity, no drawback for Vickrey, who draws effortlessly.

Even so, he finds any general description of egg tempera imprecise and urges viewers of his paintings to see these effects for themselves. Vickrey is dedicated to the medium's inherent beauty in an age when some experts find beauty not serious enough to occupy the inquiring mind beyond the superficial. With many other realists, Vickrey has long rejected this idea. He looks at the history of Western art as his guide and proof, reassuring lovers of beauty who think as he does.

But the artist is also aware of some of egg tempera's limitations. Pigments mixed with egg yolk must be

CROSSINGS, Egg tempera on gesso on panel, 20" x 30", circa 1972. *Private collection.*

applied in thin coats or they crack and peel. Because this mixture dries quickly, blending color values is far more difficult than with oils, particularly if the area to be painted is large. Also egg tempera's color range, better suited to lighter tints than darker hues, is much narrower than that of oils.

Many of Vickrey's adventures with egg tempera ranged far beyond his studio, and none more so than when he traveled for his TIME covers. Getting fresh eggs could be a problem. He once flew to Paris and waited seven days to begin a portrait of Princess Aisha of Morocco, then considered, according to TIME, "symbolic of the Arabian liberated woman."

The Princess did not deign to pose for Vickrey in Paris, then, after a week of waiting, he and TIME writer Bill McHale followed her by plane to Rabat, the Moroccan capital. Vickrey settled into a French Quarter hotel and waited four more days to be summoned. When finally called, Vickrey was ready with his paint and panel. All he needed was an egg.

Picking up the telephone, he ordered, "Two eggs—uh, deux oeufs—um, not cooked" from room service. "Oui, Monsieur," room service said. And shortly Vickrey was presented with two soft-boiled eggs. "No," he called down, "not cooked, pas cooked." Voila! Two more eggs, less well-done this time, appeared. He called a third time and was told, "We close now."

McHale arrived to say the limousine was waiting. "Quick!" said Vickrey, "Where's the nearest grocery store?"

"They're all closed," McHale said. "Everything here closes in the middle of the day. But wait, the bar stays open. They must have eggs for daiquiris and things." They hurried down to the bar. The bartender looked like the French actor Fernandel. McHale negotiated with him in French with much arm-waving.

"What's going on?" Vickrey asked.

"He has eggs but he's not allowed to sell us one."

"Tell him it's for the princess," Vickrey said. The bartender showed Gallic disbelief.

"Tell him it's to mix the paint with," Vickrey continued.

BIRD WALL, Egg tempera on gesso panel, 20″ x 30″, 1974. *Private Collection.* The bas-relief in the background is based on a series of walls in New York's Central Park. Vandals over the decades have smashed and broken the birds, which now resemble diving bombers. The innocent pinecones have become the hand grenades of war.

"Your limousine is waiting," the doorman called.

McHale tried one more time. "Ahh," said the bartender, beaming with sudden understanding and with a little flourish, presented a single ovoid.

"What did you tell him?" Vickrey asked.

"I told him you painted still lifes and wanted to paint a picture of an egg…not with an egg. That he was willing to believe." Years later in his studio, Vickrey ruminated, "I know now I should have asked for cru, raw, but I didn't know that then."

He finally painted the Princess even though he was not allowed to ask her to sit still. "One does not tell a princess what to do," McHale whispered.

When the story on the princess appeared in TIME, there was a brief account of the artist's experience on the contents page and a photograph of Vickrey painting the princess. But, his wife noticed, while he finally had a photograph of himself in the magazine, he was snapped with his shirttail out.

The Morocco story illustrates a disadvantage of egg tempera—eggs aren't always available. Other artists, Vickrey learned, encountered similar problems. As a correspondent in World War II, artist Peter Hurd, Andrew Wyeth's late brother-in-law, was unable to find eggs for his paintings. He thought of the same solution he used for his nutritional needs and mixed powdered eggs into his pigments. Today, Vickrey will not be caught without fresh eggs. They may not always be in his kitchen, but they are usually in his studio refrigerators.

Vickrey's outstanding abilities with his medium earned him an accolade from the late John Canaday. The often acerbic NEW YORK TIMES senior art critic wrote in a 1973 review that Vickrey "must surely be the world's most proficient craftsman in egg tempera painting."

The artist received his work at TIME after an assistant managing editor saw his painting in the Whitney Museum of American Art annual and called him to do a magazine cover portrait of Christian Dior, designer of

THE LARGE KEY, Egg tempera on gesso panel, 8" x 12", circa 1974. *Private collection.*

"the New Look" that made women's hemlines longer and dresses shapelier. TIME supplied Vickrey with several photographs of Dior. The artist noted immediately the full-faced Frenchman resembled his hero, Alfred Hitchcock.

"And the longer I worked on the portrait, the more he looked like Hitchcock. I decided to show him holding a huge pair of scissors that were faintly menacing. The viewer could not be sure whether he was about to attack a bolt of cloth or a model. My editor said, 'Dior never touches shears or scissors or anything like that. But if you think it will make a good cover, go ahead and do it. We'll send you an assortment of instruments.'"

When the magazine appeared a few weeks later, Vickrey bought several copies in various locations, ostensibly to compare the printing quality, but actually to own a few more issues. He was told later in the 1960s that Dior had designed a habit for the Daughters of Charity of St. Vincent de Paul. There is no documentation of this at the House of Dior or the motherhouse today, but at the time the motherhouse promptly corrected such a story. The habit's designer was an unnamed Daughter who had worked for Dior before joining the community. When looking for a suitable design, the sisters had called on her talent and expertise, which are evident in the habits to this day. Seven sisters were questioned separately and confirmed this account.

While in Paris in 1951,Vickrey was strolling in front of Notre Dame Cathedral. He saw a Daughter in habit and cornette holding a wooden bowl and asking alms for the poor. This was well before the rumored Dior incident or the possibility he had been consulted. Vickrey has been long amused by the idea of the sisters begging in Dior originals. But as one sister has said to Sister Betty Ann McNeil, the Daughters, knowing anything designed by Dior would be expensive, would have been shocked and scandalized to be working with the poor while wearing Dior.

The artist believes fate had somehow stepped in to direct his first TIME cover just as he had begun his fascination with the Daughters. To him the coincidence has seemed for many years almost preordained.

LENGTHENING SHADOWS, Egg tempera on gesso panel,
approx 9" x 13", circa 1973. *Private collection*

MUSEUM CORRIDOR, Acrylic on paperboard, 24″ x 36″, 1974.
Private Collection.

RAINY DAY, Egg tempera on gesso panel,12" x 16", circa 1975.
Private collection.

NUN AND BICYCLE, Egg tempera on gesso panel, 8" x 10", 1976.
Private collection.

WHITE CORNER, Egg tempera on gesso panel, 8" x 10", 1980.
Private collection, Naples, FL.

GRAFFITI, Egg tempera on gesso panel, 24" x 36", 1980.
Private collection, Naples, FL.

BUTTERFLY AND
BRANCH SHADOWS,
Egg tempera on gesso
panel, 18" x 14", 1980.
Private collection,
Naples, FL.

MORPHO AEGA, Acrylic on paperboard, 39 1/4" x 28 1/2", 1980. *Private collection, Tuscaloosa, AL.* This is the Latin name of the butterfly.

REFLECTIONS AND REFRACTIONS, Oil on gesso panel, 23 1/2″ x 31″, 1982.
Collection of Mr. and Mrs. John C. Wasmer, Jr.

CURVED WALLS, Egg tempera on gesso panel, 19 1/2" x 13 1/2", 1982.
Collection of Mr. and Mrs. Arthur Hurr.

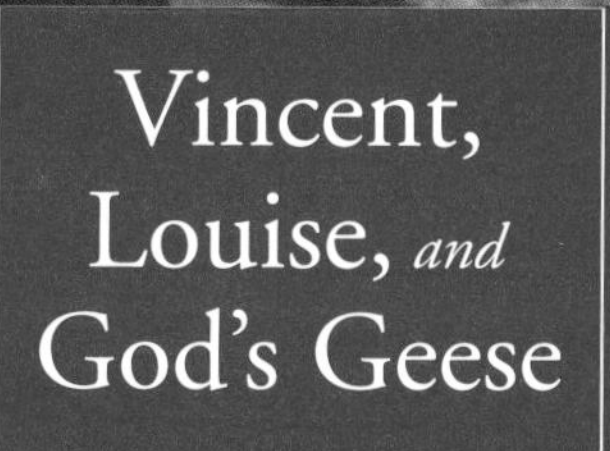

Vincent, Louise, *and* God's Geese

CHAPTER THREE

SEVENTEENTH-CENTURY FRANCE is often called splendid because of Louis XIV's glittering court and monarchical ambitions. He became king at age five in 1643 and ruled until 1715. But for the French people the century was far from good. Plagues and civil wars were devastating, crop failures frequent, and a barometer of the economy—the price of bread—could soar.

Farmers were heavily taxed but the nobility was not, sowing the seeds of resentment that would explode in 1789 with revolution and bloodshed. Peasants worked the fields barefoot or with feet wrapped in rags. Wars decimated towns. Citizens abandoned farms and villages and fled to cities for food and shelter. Those found guilty of even small crimes were force-marched in chains from Paris to Marseille and to deathly prison ships in the Mediterranean, where escape was commonly burial at sea. Galley slaves and the insane were beaten and treated worse than animals.

Harried parents and guardians often abandoned their children in the streets. Saint Vincent de Paul described their fate: "The children were sold to scoundrels who broke their arms and legs in order to arouse the compassion of passersby and incline them to give alms. The children were allowed to die of hunger and were given laudanum [opium] pills to put them to sleep without ever being baptized."

Vincent was born in Gascony, southwestern France, on April 24, 1576. He was the third child of poor parents; as a youngster he herded pigs. Vincent relished recalling this experience when others spoke pretentiously of their origins. Educated by the Franciscans at Dax and Toulouse, Vincent was ordained a priest in 1600. After visits to Avignon and Rome, he at length reached Paris, where Pierre de Berulle, an important cardinal and statesman, found him a curacy at Clichy, near Paris, in 1611. After a year or so, Vincent became tutor to the wealthy Comte de Joigny in the diocese of Amiens.

In 1617, Vincent was named curate of Châtillon-les-Domes, south of Paris. Here he began to ask people of goodwill to help the poor. He first aroused his parishioners to donate food to a sick family. So effective was his

Previous page: NUN IN THE RAIN, Acrylic on paperboard, 23 3/8" x 35 3/8", circa 1975. *Collection of the Springfield Art Museum, Springfield, MO.*

call that food and goods overwhelmed the family. These donations convinced Vincent a systematic method was needed to aid the unfortunate.

That same year, Vincent formed the first Confraternity of Charity, a group of mostly married women with domestic duties. On making sure the women handled donations efficiently, he formed more confraternities.

A keen judge of character and in his way a rebel, Vincent did not always follow conventions or the religious community's every rule. But quietly charismatic, he gained the support of wealthy patrons willing to help the poor. His success with the poor led Vincent to create "missions." In 1625, he founded the Congregation of the Mission, the order better known as the Vincentian Priests and Brothers (hence, the abbreviation "C.M." after their names, similar to the Daughters' "D.C."), who were originally assigned to minister and preach to the poor in rural areas. At the time, many former faithful, fed up with uneducated country priests, had left the church. Vincent became famous through these missions

OVAL WINDOW, Egg tempera on gesso panel, 24" x 18", 1983.
Collection of Mrs. Isobel Robinson, Naples, FL.

and his deep knowledge of the poor. He always made sure those hand-ling donations were trained and organized.

Louise de Marillac, a personable 34-year-old widow who had an adolescent son, chose Vincent as her spiritual director. He at first entrusted her with charitable work and soon sent her to Paris to observe the progress of the confraternities there.

Both Vincent and Louise found wealthy women, who joined their charitable groups, soon became disgusted with serving the poor. Louise suggested to Vincent that peasant girls, accus-

THE BOUQUET, Acrylic on paperboard, 25" x 37", 1984. *Collection of Thomas R. Quick Center for the Arts, Fairfield University, CT.*

MIDSUMMER DREAMS, Egg tempera on gesso panel, 36" x 48", 1984-5. *Private collection.* This is the first painting of mine that is derived from the work of another artist, in this case, Pieter Bruegel the Elder's "January (Hunter in the Snow)." I was interested in the contrast between summer in the foreground and winter in the background. My dog Webster is next to Bruegel's dogs. The dove in the upper right is trying to fly into a blocked up window, while the birds in the mural fly free.

EIGHT BY ONE, Egg tempera on gesso panel, approx 15" x 26", circa 1988. *Private collection in Arizona.*

tomed to hard labor, be trained to visit, nurse and feed the indigent sick. He agreed and his instruction revealed his understanding of human nature.

In the French motion picture, *Monsieur Vincent,* 1949, the future saint, says to one of the first of these peasant Daughters:

"You will find that charity is a heavy burden to carry; heavier than the kettle of soup and the basket of bread [you tote]. But you must keep your gentleness and your smile. Giving soup and bread isn't all [that must be done]; that the rich can do!"

You are the little servant of the poor, the maid of charity, always smiling and in good humor. The poor are your masters, terribly sensitive and exacting, as you will see. But the more ugly and dirty they are, the more unjust and bitter, the more you must give them of your love.

It is only because of your love—only your love—that the poor will forgive you the bread you give them."

It was as though Vincent had adapted Jesus Christ's words of charity to his own harsh age.

Vickrey owns a video-cassette of Monsieur Vincent. It has helped him to visualize what life was like in seventeenth century France—when finery often cloaked the unspeakable, when wealthy women in gorgeous gowns tottered about on high heels performing the unpleasant task of caring for the poor.

The artist knows another example illustrating such a time. A French painting—untitled, unsigned and probably from the last quarter of the nineteenth century—hangs in the house of the Daughters of Charity in St. Georges de Lisle, Rennes, France. It depicts two sisters in habits and cornettes bending to give food to urchins who lie starving and derelict in a stone street.

Vincent and Louise de Marillac co-founded the Daughters of Charity of St. Vincent de Paul on November 29, 1633. Louise had brought young women into her home to prepare them for apostolic service in a community. A shepherdess, thirty-six-year-old Marguerite Naseau (1594-1633), was the first Daughter; soon three more women joined her. But Marguerite would die prematurely, having tried to comfort a plague victim by sleeping in her bed. Many different congregations of Sisters of Charity follow rules based on St. Vincent. For instance, the

American Sisters of Charity of St. Joseph's, founded by St. Elizabeth Ann Seton in 1809 in Emmitsburg, Maryland, became affiliated with the Daughters of Charity of St. Vincent de Paul in 1850, assuming their habit and cornette.

It was nothing short of revolutionary in the seventeenth century for religious women to work among the people. The Daughters were the first non-cloistered religious women to do this. Although nuns had operated schools and hospitals before this, such activities had always occurred behind convent walls.

Vincent, seeking freedom of movement for the Daughters, asked them to avoid dressing like nuns or even calling themselves members of a religious order, since the word "religious" then meant enclosure. For many years he would not permit Daughters to take religious vows, fearing that if they did, they would be forced into confinement. They were, and still are, called Sisters, not nuns, and live in a "house" rather than a convent. Their leader is called "Sister Servant," not Superior, and they join together as a "company" and not as an order. Originally, the Daughters wore no religious garments, but only the simple clothing of country women.

Their dressing style has varied considerably over the centuries. Before 1685, Daughters wore a gray gabardine dress and a white linen toque that fit the head closely and covered the hair—the way women living near the French capital usually dressed. But this small cap gave scant protection from the cold.

The Daughters complained to Vincent that even peasant women wore a kind of sunbonnet for protection from the elements. He agreed that cornettes could be worn as long as they were uniform. Since nearly all of the first postulants (candidates) were from Paris' suburbs, Vincent allowed them their ordinary dress, and those who came later from other parts of the country adopted it.

Superiors denied Daughters any personal innovations to habits, except those suggested for health reasons, particularly warmth; but even then always within bounds. Vincent could not decide to let Louise de Marillac dress like her Daughters. When she could no longer endure the indecision, she went on Whitsunday 1639 to the parish church dressed as simply as they, covering her head with a white linen coif like those poor women in delicate health wore. She fell ill and needed a long time to recover.

Still, Louise somehow forgot this setback, and toward the end of that, took a long journey to Angers in northwestern France to establish a hospital. Putting aside her veil and gloves to harden herself to the cold, she again became ill. But this time she convinced herself that any further privation of this kind was only tempting fate.

After the pain from leaving her face and head exposed had vanished, Louise received Vincent's permission for Sisters with recently cut hair to wear the linen coif she had tried. But this change allowed for so many exceptions to the rules, and so many heads suffered from the weather, that in 1685 the uniform cornette became mandatory. This covering had little resemblance to later cornettes. In the early years, ends drooped down as far as the shoulders. Only in 1750—and later helped by heavy starching—did cornette wings start to unfold and expand.

Vincent was a stickler on uniformity. He noted Sisters under superiors' eyes in Paris did not dare to follow their dress whims, but those in the country easily found little ways to smarten themselves.

"If this be not taken in hand," he said, "you will see them with a dress cut now in one style and now in another, with finer linen, a neater headdress, and then they will begin to let their hair appear." But only a few succumbed to this. Generally, Sisters were quite content with the poor and simple dress supplied to them. In this way they attracted less attention, which helped to safeguard them. But there was still danger in those perilous times. Vincent forbade Sisters to go out alone, converse with men in the streets or allow men in parts of houses reserved for Sisters.

MADISON AVENUE HAWK, Oil on panel, 20" x 28", 1985.
Private collection.

Beneath the cornette, Daughters wore white linen collars and bi-forked squared bibs, much like the rest of European female laity. From 1685 to 1760, their head covering resembled a loose kerchief falling to the shoulders. They were not alone in these matters.

Johannes Vermeer (1632-1675) immortalized such a shawl in his oil painting on canvas *Woman Holding a Balance,* about 1664, Widener Collection, National Gallery of Art, Washington, D.C. Some Daughters of Charity believe Vermeer's painting of *The Kitchen Maid,* c. 1658, resembles how Marguerite Naseau, the first Daughter, must have looked. The European woman's headdress has an extremely long fashion history. Rogier van der Weyden depicted a more diaphanous version almost two hundred years earlier in *Portrait of a Lady,* oil on panel, about 1460, Andrew W. Mellon Collection, National Gallery of Art, Washington, D.C.

Much later, during and after the 1870's, French Naturalist artists, as well as European-influenced Americans and others, loved to paint Breton peasant women in their bonnets that were both elaborate and quaint. Vincent van Gogh (1853-90) depicted two impoverished Netherlandish women in dust caps in *The Potato-Eaters,* 1885, National Museum Vincent van Gogh, Amsterdam.

Paul Gauguin (1848-1903) created the most important depiction of peasant headdresses in modern art with *The Vision After the Sermon,* also known as *Jacob Wrestling with the Angel,* 1888, National Gallery of Scotland, Edinburgh. In this painting

NUN UNDER STAIRWAY, Oil on panel, 24″ x 16″, 1986.
Private collection, Minneapolis, MN.

TRILOGY REFLECTIONS,
Oil on gesso panel,
16" x 22", 1986.
Private collection,
Bethesda, MD.

unsophisticated Breton women imagine the vision that Gauguin indicates with a non-naturalistic red foreground. This work marked Gauguin's break with naturalistic Impressionism.

In the not too distant past of some of us, the bonnet could be found in American kitchens on "Old Dutch Cleanser" cans. A girl in wooden shoes, deep white bonnet that covered her profile and holding an upright stick chased unseen dirt around the powder-dispensing cylinder.

After 1760, the Daughters' kerchief became stiff, concealed the ears and was folded in two triangles on either side of the head. These linen cornettes had to be washed and soaked in the heaviest starch. They were then laid flat and smoothed out in rectangular tin molds and allowed to dry. When stiff, they were folded into their distinctive shape and pinned to close-fitting white caps covering the hair.

By 1804, this covering had grown larger, hanging down from the back and projecting stiffly from the temples. A short time later appeared the grand cornette Robert Vickrey so admires. Specially constructed with large white wings stretching outward into the air, this cornette is to Vickrey the most beautiful shape in the world: "Much better than a David Smith sculpture."

So even though this lovely form appears to have come down directly from medieval times, it evolved over a long period. The final version was in use for one hundred and sixty years, including on the battlefield at Gettysburg. When in modern times the beautifully designed but heavy gabardine wool two-piece habit and flaring cornette became burdensome, the entire ensemble was relegated to the past. A more practical, though less picturesque, garment would replace it.

When beginning in France, the Daughters first treated the poor and ill in their houses, then at Paris' Hotel Dieu. Vincent was actively involved with this large public hospital. Growing in numbers and influence, the

SILENT WINGS, Egg tempera on gesso panel, 30 1/2" x 20 1/2", 1988. *Private collection.*

Daughters fostered hundreds of abandoned children annually as well as continuing to help the poor and ill, feeding and washing the clothes of galley slaves and caring for the mentally ill. Founding the motherhouse at 140 Rue du Bac, literally "Street of the Ferryboat," on the Left Bank, the Daughters soon established schools and hospitals that helped thousands of people.

Both Vincent and Louise died in Paris in 1660. Louise passed away on March 15 and her remains repose in the Motherhouse's Chapel of the Miraculous Medal. Vincent died on September 27 and is enshrined one block away in Paris' Church of St. Lazare, both locations on the Left Bank. They had worked together for thirty-five years, and saw the community of Daughters grow to fifty-one houses and three hundred members. St. Vincent de Paul was canonized in 1737 and St. Louise de Marillac in 1934. Under the tutelage of Rosalie Rindu, a Daughter of Charity, Frédéric Ozanam and others founded the charitable Society of St. Vincent de Paul in 1833.

By the start of the French Revolution in 1789, the Daughters had established four hundred and thirty communities in France, twenty in Poland, and one in Spain. The French Revolution's anti-religious fervor claimed the lives of ten Daughters and the suppression of their communities. Hostilities ended with the turn of the eighteenth century. The original motherhouse was near the convent of St. Lazare, a converted leper colony St. Vincent had overseen in Paris' parish of St. Laurent. It was so revered that French kings' funeral processions stopped there for blessing en route to burial in the Cathedral of St. Denis, first church in the Gothic style. Both the original motherhouse and the convent were destroyed in the revolution. In 1815, The Daughters of Charity

GHOSTS, Egg tempera on gesso panel, 20" x 27", 1988. *Private collection.*

established the present motherhouse at 140 Rue du Bac, in English "Ferryboat Street," also on the Left Bank, creating schools and hospitals that have helped thousands of needy. Shortly after the French Daughters had reorganized their communities, Elizabeth Ann Seton, who founded the Sisters of Charity of St. Joseph's, embraced the philosophy of Sts. Vincent and Louise. St. Elizabeth founded the first group of religious women and the first free Catholic school for girls in the United States in Emmitsburg, Maryland, on July 31, 1809. From the St. Joseph's Valley there, the Daughters of Charity of St. Vincent de Paul fanned out to help the poor along the Eastern seaboard and into America's little known interior.

Six Daughters left Emmitsburg for San Francisco, California, in 1852. They took a sailing ship to the Isthmus of Panama and crossed it by mule. Two Daughters died from the rigors of the journey. A later group boarded another ship and three months later came ashore from a longboat at San Pedro, California, on January 6, 1856. They then climbed onto a Banning stagecoach for the bumpy ten-hour trip to the pueblo of Los Angeles, inhabited by fewer than 6,000 people.

This is how the Daughters operate. They are not subject to a local diocese. With Vatican approval, Daughters assume responsibility for their own activities but serve wherever feasible to address unmet human needs within dioceses.

By 1991, there were 3,132 local community houses internationally. Four provinces are in Africa, five in North America, nineteen in Latin America, six in Asia, thirty-nine in Europe and one in Oceania. By 2000, the Vatican numbered Daughters at 24,982 living in 2,757 local communities worldwide. Population decline is attributed to women's changing roles and different ideas of public service. Today, Daughters make up the largest society of apostolic women.Their service in wars earned Daughters the title "Angels of the Battlefield." Two hundred and seventy served in the Civil War and sixty were nurses in the 1863 Battle of Gettysburg. They have also been called "God's geese," for the way they appeared when walking or gathering together in their former habits and cornettes. Robert Vickrey has often captured this sight in his paintings.

Around the globe, 45,000 Daughters put aside their historic garb on September 20, 1964. Each sister then donned a simpler headdress and shorter dress. Removing the stiff cornette and blue serge robe ended, in one day, a tradition that had lasted three centuries. Many old and worn habits were burned, but others were recycled into clothing for needy children. Today, many Daughters' archives treasure them as artifacts. The Daughters had decidedly mixed feelings on leaving these garments behind. Older nuns may still miss the cornette and younger ones who never wore it respect its symbolism. But there will be no turning back.

For many, the cornette was a symbol of protection to those under its shadow. Strange tales have been attributed to the habit. Daughters have told Vickrey that straight pins holding the bonnet fast to the head had significance and V-shaped seams in its back and those inverted in the habit's rear reminded them of St. Vincent.

Sister Betty Ann McNeil, archivist at St. Joseph's Provincial House in Emmitsburg, has found that the straight pins were mostly functional. But one in the top center of the cornette was called the "obedience pin." When a seminary sister received her habit, the pin was inserted to signify the mutual bonds between the Sister's service of authority and commitment to obedience.

"I don't paint the pins," Vickrey said, "because when I did, people thought they were scratches on the paintings." But he is still fascinated by the sisterly legends, wondering how they came about and how many there are. At the same time, Sister Betty Ann McNeil is determined to end as many false ones as she can. Daughters don't need questionable legends. The traditional ones are sufficiently vivid.

Yet almost forty years after it was set aside, the cornette remains a popular image of the Daughters of Charity. Vickrey, with his paintings, has done all he can to keep its memory alive.

AFTER THE FESTIVITIES, Egg tempera on gesso panel, 25 1/2" x 31 1/2", 1989. *Collection of Mr. & Mrs. Dolph von Arx.* This is a satire on the joyless activities of Bouguereau's nymphs. My two nuns are quite sensibly going in the opposite direction.

BOULEVARD DES CAPUCINES,
Egg tempera on gesso panel,
16″ x 12″, 1990. *Private collection.*

CLAUDE'S NUNS, Egg tempera on gesso panel, 20" x 24", 1990. After Monet's *Avenue des Capucines.* *Private collection.*

ROUSSEAU NEGATIVE, Egg tempera on gesso panel, " 9" x 12", 1990. *Private collection.* Rousseau Negative and Positive depict the same painting with the darks and lights reversed. The colors in one are represented by the color negatives in the other—two views of life.

ROUSSEAU POSITIVE,
Egg tempera on gesso panel, 18" x 12", 1990.
Private collection, Naples, FL.

VENETIAN DREAMS, Egg tempera on gesso panel, 8 1/2″ x 12″, 1990. *Collection of Mr. & Mrs. J. William Meek, III, Naples, FL.*

GONDOLAS AND BALLOONS, Egg tempera on gesso panel, 12″ x 16″, 1991. *Private collection.*

BUTTERFLIES AND NUN, Egg tempera on gesso panel, 20" x 28", 1992. *Private collection.*

COOL CORNER, Egg tempera on gesso panel, 12 1/2" x 17 1/2", 1992. *Private collection.*

SHADOW PLAY, Oil on gesso panel, 32" x 47", 1993. *Private collection.*

WHITE ON WHITE, Egg tempera on gesso panel, 20" x 28", 1992. *Collection of Mr. & Mrs. Dolph von Arx.*

Coming Together

CHAPTER FOUR

Chapter 4: *Coming Together*

IT IS IMPOSSIBLE TO KNOW what impact over the years Robert Vickrey's nun paintings have had on the public, but there are accounts of it. None is more vivid than that of Sister Mary Walter Boyle, a Boston native and Daughter of Charity of St. Vincent de Paul. Like Vickrey, Sister is in her seventh decade.

A supervisor at Boston's Carney Hospital for many years, Sr. Mary Walter now lives in the St. Vincent's Residence, Bridgeport, Connecticut. She recently oversaw the installation of one hundred and twenty-five beds in a new hospital in Sarajevo, Bosnia. Her interest in the nun paintings is a long one.

"I found Robert Vickrey in 1988," she recalled. " I had seen his work and had the greatest desire to meet him. From Carney Hospital I drove down to the Cape with the hospital's director of development. In Orleans, I got out the phone book and called him. I went for a ride and found him at Crystal Lake. I wasn't dressed in my old habit. I think he expected me in full regalia."

In Vickrey's studio, Sister Mary Walter spied a doll the artist had used in *Remnants,* a painting of broken dolls that symbolized the Nazi death camps. The doll had belonged to Vickrey's daughter and its hand was broken. Sister asked to borrow the doll.

"I had early sewing experience from my mother," she said, "and back in Boston I designed a habit for the doll down to the last detail." Since Sister didn't have any old drying molds, she pressed the starched miniature cornette evenly on the side of a refrigerator. "After a long search, we finally found a craftsman who was able to repair the hand. The doll, dressed in habit and cornette, was given to Vickrey. The whole experience took three years".

Sometime after that, Sister Mary Walter talked with another Daughter of Charity, Sister Anna Walkaukas, now of the provincial house in Albany, New York, that still preserves an authentic habit and cornette. Sister Anna had appeared in the habit on a parade float celebrating the Carney Hospital's history in an annual parade

Previous page: SEA BREEZE, Oil on panel,
20 1/4" x 30 1/4", 1985.
Collection of the Boca Raton Museum of Art, FL.

ELEVEN SHADOWS,
Egg tempera on gesso panel, 8" x 12", 1993.
Private collection.

in its Boston neighborhood of Dorchester. "I thought Sister Anna would make an excellent model for Bob," Sister Mary Walter said, "so we drove down to his studio. He was so disappointed when he saw we weren't wearing our habits. But we said, 'Just lend us a bedroom!' and we put on our old habits. Bob asked me to make a typical gesture that we would do when we wore the cornette. I knew that when its wings went up in the wind we would gently reach up and pull them down. Bob took a lot of pictures. It was a delightful experience." For posing purposes, Vickrey assembled ten large sheets of styrofoam to simulate a nun's cell.

WINDSWEPT,
Egg tempera on gesso panel,
8" x 12", 1994.
Private collection, Naples, FL.

Sister Mary Boyle told how she came to her profession. "I was born in Boston but lived my early years in New Hampshire. Once when I was a cadet nurse I visited a friend who had died. In the funeral home I saw two sisters wearing cornettes.

"I was sixteen years old then and interested in boys. I said to myself, when I graduate, I am going to go to those nuns' hospital. It was the Carney Hospital." Later, in 1950, after her early years in nursing school, she had an insistent calling to become a nun and she made her vows for the first time in 1955. Every March 25, on the Feast Day of the Annunciation, when the Archangel Gabriel told Mary she was to be the Mother of the Son of God, Sister Mary Walter and all of the other Daughters renew those vows for another year.

For years, as a nurse on hospital duty, Mary Walter wore a long white gown and cornette to work. After work, she would change into her regular habit. "It was made of heavy French wool and weighed twelve pounds. Each Daughter made her own habit, although later they were manufactured. We made our habits for the first fourteen years I was a Daughter. We would use graph paper to get the pleats right around the waist and then would put a heavy thread through it to pull it together.

"The habit was very, very beautiful! But for those Daughters who couldn't sew, making the robe was their greatest penance! And after we washed and starched our linen cornettes—the special heavy starch came from Belgium—we would lay them out in tin molds so they would dry evenly. They were wonderful but it was difficult getting into a small automobile with one on. It's amazing to me that they were worn for three hundred years and then, in a moment, were gone. I guess they had their day, but I think there isn't one Daughter who would not love to wear one again."

Vickrey, expressing his somewhat saturnine turn of mind in the film *Robert Vickrey—Lyrical Realist* said he believes cornettes were just too beautiful to last in this world. Since he called his own work "dreamscapes" in the film, it is possible that the cornette reminds him of his own status as "a realist lost in the contemporary art world. My test for a painting is not what style is it but is it any good. A painting is good for me if it works."

"Because of our friendship," Sister Mary Walter recalled, "Bob Vickrey did a nun painting for me. He said, 'What do you want for the background?' I said, 'I love the water. Please put sailboats in the background.' And he did. There is another Vickrey painting in the provincial house in Albany, New York."

Sister Mary Walter remembered from history that both Saints Vincent and Louise were known at the French court. "Both worked with rich people and understood their ways as well as those of the poor." She totally agrees with St. Vincent's admonition to love the poor. "My whole life has been wonderful." One would not doubt that she is joyful.

Robert Vickrey learned that a Daughter was permitted to wear a habit when she appeared in a Boston parade. "I was thrilled when Sister Mary Walter appeared at my door and said that her friend, Sister Anna, wanted to pose in her habit for me. I took photographs of them both in the habits, but I was not able to control the sunlight. Later I did a painting of the doll dressed in the habit in a tennis court. I made a paper stencil that created the effect of leafy shadow patterns in the painting. Actually, my daughters have posed for most of the nun paintings.

"At one point I constructed a large, almost three-foot-wide cornette of white cardboard. I wanted my daughters' faces to be in an actual cornette. I liked to have a little light come through to the face. That doesn't happen in real life. I also made three smaller cornettes. I tried several to see how the light fell on them but it didn't work too well.

"Still, with time, I was able to work on multiple versions of paintings, finding variations, seemingly endless, on a theme. I was surprised to find, when I unfolded the cardboard cornettes after cutting along their angles,

SEVEN WINGS, Egg tempera on gesso panel, 15″ x 21″, 1994. *Private collection.*

they formed perfect rectangles just like the real ones."

The shadowed or patterned nun paintings are frequently done in blue and gray with white highlights. "For 'Wings,' my daughter Carri posed in a cardboard cornette I made," Vickrey said. "It was inaccurate. But when I used the doll wearing the habit, the paintings became accurate. It was a matter of evolving."

Cecropia Moths is a nun painting that shows these insects in mid-flight, as though they were butterflies, which Vickrey also frequently depicts as enigmatic symbols of freedom as well as fragile, short-lived messengers of beauty. He has noted that people prefer butterflies to moths.

As Philip Eliasoph wrote in his 1995 catalogue, "Vickrey has examined the nun's recognizable silhouette in an infinite variety of poses. Viewed from directly above, they look like a phalanx of white sail boats in a regatta;

in a lateral depiction they appear as their lovely nickname 'God's geese,' gliding in front of a decaying tenement wall." The illusions are as varied as the paintings' subjects and continue to pour forth from the studios.

Robert Vickrey believes his largest painting in this series is *Study of Nun with Posters,* 1957-92, at four by six feet. The posters seem to intermingle with the cornette. In FEAR, a nun runs through an open field trying to escape modernity. The Sara Roby Foundation donated it to the National Museum of American Art. It is a natural successor to *Labyrinth.*

The artist has always loved the Staten Island ferry and has set many paintings on board. It is a coincidence that the Daughters' motherhouse is on the Left Bank's "Ferryboat Street." He is particularly entranced by the reflections, sense of motion and separation in space and teeming boaters. He recalls being so broke as a Yale student taking his date back and forth on the ferry in the dark and it only cost five cents. His date would one day become his second wife. He would later take his children for ferry rides and used the boat in one of his films that, like his paintings, incorporated movement, light and reflections.

Vickrey's mind is a carousel of painting images, some of which are incorporated in paintings where the nuns may stroll in the background of a painting after Georges Seurat's *La Grande Jatte* called *La Jatte*

BLUE EPIPHANY,
Acrylic on paperboard,
28" x 37", 1995.
Private Collection.

Aujourd 'hui, or luscious sirens from William Adophe Bouguereau, with both artists' works depicted uncharacteristically on urban brick walls. Vickrey loves this visual badminton with art historical imagery, not so far removed from his actual tennis games.

More recent works show a nun standing beneath seemingly molten color that is cast on the walls by artist Dale Chihuly's sixty-foot-long glass installation *Persian Ceiling* in Southwest Florida's Naples Museum of Art. Another painting depicts a tiny nun, hardly larger than a speck, hurrying toward American architect Frank Gehry's Solomon R. Guggenheim Museum in Bilbao, Spain. *(See page 82.)* When it comes to his favorite subject, there is little chance the artist will ever run out of ideas.

"Sister Mary Walter took the doll from the studio in 1990 and I got it back about three years later," he recalled. "I decided I would have a box made for it with a glass front to protect it from the dust."

And so in Robert Vickrey's Orleans studio, the bright-faced doll in her blue habit and white cornette stands in her case. Like a real Daughter, she is ever ready to serve as more nun paintings flow from the artist's brush and imagination.

SUNLIT NUN, Egg tempera on gesso panel, 15 1/2" x 23", 1995. *Collection of Ann and Arthur Ferguson.*

LA JATTE AUJOURD 'HUI, Egg tempera on gesso panel, 28" x 40", 1995. *Private collection.*
I wanted to depict Seurat's famous scene as it might look today. The elegant lady in the foreground of Seurat's painting has been left deserted and pregnant by her top-hatted friend, while behind her we see a mugging, the shark from *Jaws*, the Lochness Monster, polluting factories, E.T., and my two favorite innocent nuns.

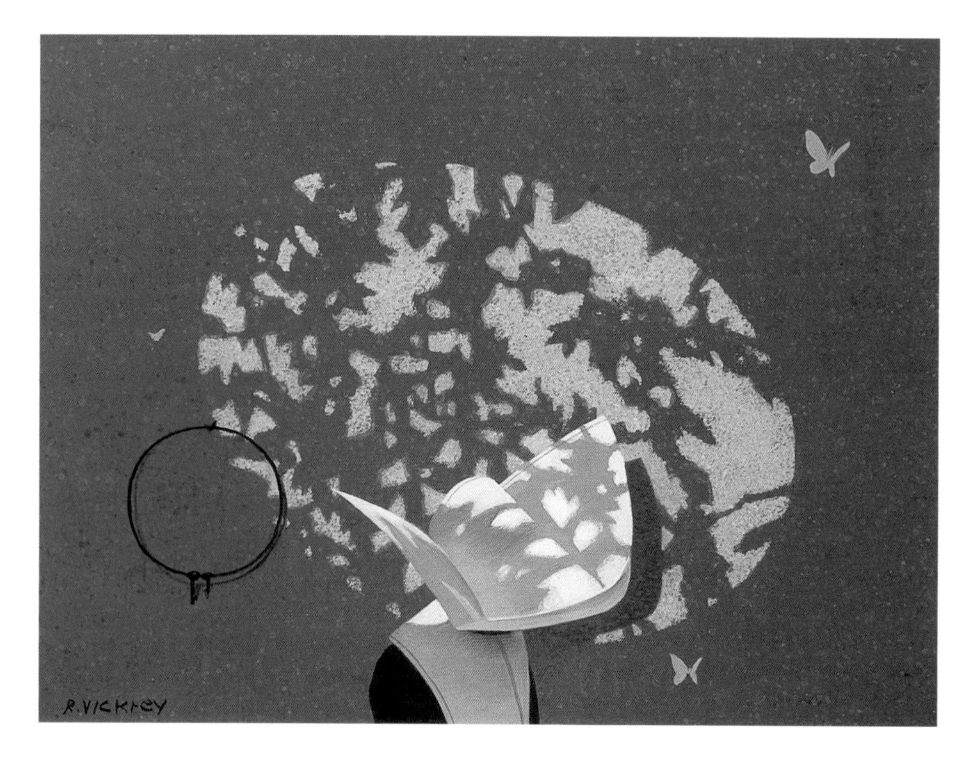

SISTER ESTHER, Egg tempera on gesso panel, 8″ x 10″, 1998. *Collection of Martin and Melanie Wasmer..*

CORNERED, Egg tempera on gesso panel, 9″ x 12″, 1998. *Collection of Mr. & Mrs. John C. Wasmer, Jr.*

VENETIAN PUPPET SHOP, Egg tempera on gesso panel, 20" x 16", 1999. *Private collection, Naples, FL.* In Venice I saw several shop windows full of puppets and marionettes which seemed to represent the various follies of mankind. The nun in the foreground seems to despair of all this.

BANYAN BANSHEES, Egg tempera on gesso panel, 9" x 7", 1999. *Private collection, Naples, Fl.*

BILBAO BALLOONS, Egg tempera on gesso panel, 6" x 8", 2001. *Private collection, Naples, FL. Nun in Bilbao,* Ghery's museum in Bilbao is certainly the world's largest piece of sculpture, so I decided to paint it into my smallest nun painting.

CHIHULY CORRIDOR, Egg tempera on gesso panel, 4" x 6", 2001. *Collection of Myra Janco Daniels.* I am fascinated by the glass works of Dale Chihuly, and so I imagined what one of my nuns would look like in the maze of reflected lights cast by one of his pieces.

TORCELLO SHADOWS, Egg tempera on gesso panel, 20" x 23 1/2", 2001. *Collection of the College of St. Catherine, Saint Paul, Minnesota.*

LIGHT SPANGLES, Egg tempera on gesso panel, 24″ x 28″, 2001. *Private collection, Naples, FL.*

ANGELS OF VENICE, Egg tempera on gesso panel, 16″ x 12″, 2001. *Private collection, Orchard Park, NY.*

TILES OF VENICE, Egg tempera on gesso panel,
19" x 28", 2001. *Private collection.*

VENETIAN CORRIDORS, Egg tempera on gesso panel, 12" x 15", 2001. *Private collection, Naples FL.*

VENETIAN BICYCLES, Egg tempera on gesso panel, 18” x 20”, 2001.
Collection of Mr. & Mrs. William T. McCormick, Jr., Naples, FL.

NINE ANGELS, Egg tempera on gesso panel,
18″ x 24″, 2001-2. *Private collection, Naples, FL.*

DAUGHTERS THREE, Egg tempera on gesso panel,
18″ x 20″, 2001-2. *Private collection, Atlanta, GA.*

Chapter I

"Robert Vickrey: Imaginary Realities, A Retrospective of Forty-Five Years Organized by the Harmon-Meek Gallery, Naples, Florida." Catalog by Philip Eliasoph, 1995, p. 15. Miller interview with Vickrey, February 2000. "Lyrical realist" was chosen by Philip Eliasoph for a 1982 Vickrey touring exhibition and a 1982 film "Robert Vickrey—Lyrical Realist," produced by Fairfield University, Fairfield, Conn.

"Realism and Realities: The Other Side of American Painting," 1940-1960. Greta Berman, guest curator; Jeffrey Wechsler, senior curator, The Jane Voorhees Zimmerli Art Museum, Rutgers University, New Brunswick, N.J., 1981.

"The Illustrated Dictionary of Art & Artists." David Piper. Random House, New York, N.Y. 1984. Comment to Philip Eliasoph. "Robert Vickrey: Imaginary Realities," 1995 catalogue, Harman-Meek Gallery, Naples, Fla., p. 53.

Barbara Haskell, lecture on American modern art before 1945, Daniels Pavilion, Naples Museum of Art, December 4, 2000.

Chapter 2

"Caritas Christi: The Daughters of Charity of St. Vincent de Paul; 150 Years of Service to Detroit." Eleanor Luedtke, editor/writer. Providence Hospital and Medical Center and the St. Vincent and Sarah Fisher Center, Southfield, Mich. 1994.

"Egg Tempera and the Old Masters," from *New Techniques in Egg Tempera.* Robert Vickrey and Diane Cochrane. Watson-Guptill, 1973, p. 18.

"Painting the Princess," *The Affable Curmudgeon* by Robert Vickrey. Parnassus Imprints, Orleans, Mass., 1983, pp. 27-30.

Ibid. "My First TIME Cover," pp. 12-14.

“Robert Vickrey: Imaginary Realities. A Retrospective of Forty-Five Years.” Organized by the Harmon-Meek Gallery, Naples, Fla. Catalogue by Philip Eliasoph, 1995.

A sister with extensive international experience who worked with the French Daughters corroborates the non-Dior information.

Chapter 3

For painting in Rennes, France, see dust jacket of “Caritas Christi: The Daughters of Charity of St. Vincent de Paul; 150 Years of Service to Detroit.” (See first reference in Chapter II notes.)

“The Life and Works of St. Vincent de Paul,” Pierre Coste, C.M., The Newman Press, Westminster, Md., 1952. Vol. II, pp. 174, 208, 510; Vol. XIII, p. 554. Reprinted with translation by Joseph Leonard, C.M., The New City Press, Brooklyn, N.Y., 1987. Louise de Marillac, Sa Vie, Ses Virtus, Son Esprit. Unidentified author, possibly an anonymous Daughter of Charity or Vincentian priest/brother. Bruges, Belgium, 1886. Vol. 1 (of IV), p. 228.

Population figures 2000: Annuario Pontificio, The Vatican, Rome, Italy.

Based on conversations with Sister Betty Ann McNeil, archivist and mission services, St. Joseph's Provincial House, Emmitsburg, Md., and Sister Mary Walter Boyle, Vincentian Residences, Bridgeport, Conn. Daughters' California trip description, on card honoring the painting “The Arrival” by California artist Jean Appleton, St. Vincent Medical Center, Los Angeles, Calif.

Chapter 4

“From Robert Vickrey—Lyrical Realist,” 1986. Co-produced and co-directed by Richard Camp, Philip Eliasoph and Scott Vickrey, the artist's elder son, it was a CINE Golden Eagle winner, 1986. 28 minutes, 30 seconds. Sponsored by Fairfield University, Fairfield, Conn.

BOOKS BY ROBERT VICKREY

New Techniques in Egg Tempera. With Diane Cochrane. Watson-Guptill Publications, New York, N.Y. 1973

Artist at Work: Advanced Techniques in Egg Tempera Painting. Watson-Guptill Publications, New York, N.Y. 1979

The Affable Curmudgeon. Parnassus Imprints, Orleans, Mass. 1987

Cape Cod's Cockiest Crook, or Con Man's Carnival. Crystal Associates, Orleans, Mass. 1996

SOLO EXHIBITIONS

Robert Vickrey has had more than fifty solo exhibitions in fine art galleries since 1951, over half of which were at major galleries in New York City. He has also had solo exhibitions since 1959 in more than forty five art museums from coast to coast.

SANTORINI VISITOR, Egg tempera on gesso panel, 15 1/2" x 22", 1987-2002. *Private collection, Naples, FL.*

SELECTED PUBLIC COLLECTIONS

American Academy & Institute of Arts & Letters, New York, NY
Atlanta University, Atlanta, GA
Boca Raton Museum of Art, FL
Brooklyn Museum of Art, New York, NY
The Butler Institute of American Art, Youngstown, OH
Canajoharic Library & Art Gallery, Washington, D.C.
Canton Art Museum, OH
Cape Museum of Fine Arts, Dennis, MA
Chrysler Museum, Norfolk, VA
Colorado Springs Fine Arts Center, CO
Corcoran Gallery of Art, Washington, D.C.
Dallas Museum of Art, Dallas, TX
Detroit Institute of Arts, Detroit, MI
Everson Museum, Syracuse, NY
Fairfield University, CT
Fayetteville Museum of Art, NC
Finch College, MA
Florida Southern College, Lakeland, FL
Frye Art Museum, Seattle, WA
Gibbes Art Gallery, Charleston, SC
Hunter Museum of Art, Chattanooga, TN
Herbert F. Johnson Museum, Cornell University, Ithaca, NY
The High Museum of Art, Atlanta, GA
Indianapolis Museum of Art, Indianapolis, IN
Joslyn Art Museum, Omaha, NE
Kalamazoo Institute of Art, Kalamazoo, MI
Kresge Art Museum, University of Michigan, Ann Arbor, MI
Maier Museum of Art, Randolph-Macon Woman's College, Lynchburg, VA
Mattatuck Museum, Waterbury, CT
Meadows Museum, Southern Methodist University, Dallas, TX
Memphis Brooks Museum of Art, Memphis, TN

Memorial Art Gallery, University of Rochester, NY
The Metropolitan Museum of Art, New York, NY
Montgomery Museum of Fine Arts, AL
Munson-Williams-Proctor Institute, Utica, NY
Museum of Modern Art, Rio de Janeiro, Brazil
Naples Museum of Art, Naples, FL
National Academy of Design, New York, NY
National Air & Space Museum, Smithsonian Institution,Washington, D.C.
Newark Museum, NJ
New Britain Museum of American Art, CT
New Jersey State Museum, Trenton, NJ
New Orleans Museum of Art, LA
New York Cultural Center, New York, NY
Oklahoma Art Museum, Oklahoma City, OK
Parrish Art Museum, Southampton, NY
Philbrook Art Center, Tulsa, OK
Philharmonic Center for the Arts and Naples Museum of Art, Naples, FL
Polk Museum of Art, Lakeland, FL
Princeton Museum, NJ
San Diego Museum of Art, CA
Sheldon Swope Art Museum, Terre Haute, IN
Smithsonian American Art Museum, Washington, DC
Spelman College, NY
Springfield Art Museum, MO
Stedman Art Gallery, Rutgers University, Camden, NJ
Syracuse University, Syracuse, NY
Tamarind Institute, Albuquerque, NM
University of Arizona, Tucson, AZ
University of Kansas, Lawrence, KS
University of Wyoming Art Museum, Laramie, WO
Virginia Museum of Fine Arts, Richmond, VA
Wake Forest University, IL
Whitney Museum of American Art, New York, NY
Wichita Art Museum, KS
William Benton Museum of Art, University of Connecticut, Storrs, CT

GAUDI PERSPECTIVES, Egg tempera on gesso panel, 20" x 23 1/2", 2001.
Private collection, Seattle, WA.

CATALOGUE OF COLOR PLATES

After the Festivities, Egg tempera on gesso panel, 25 1/2" x 31 1/2", 1989. Collection of Mr. & Mrs. Dolph von Arx. Photo: Tim Stamm. 61

Angels of Venice, Egg tempera on gesso panel, 16" x 12", 2001. Private collection, Orchard Park, NY. Photo: Tim Stamm. 84, bottom

Banyan Banshees, Egg tempera on gesso panel, 9" x 7", 1999. Private collection, Naples, FL. Photo: Tim Stamm. 81, left

Bilbaou Balloons, Egg tempera on gesso panel, 6" x 8", 2001. Private collection, Naples, FL. 82, top

Bird Wall, Egg tempera on gesso panel, 20" x 30", 1974. Private Collection. 35

Blue Epiphany, Acrylic on paperboard, 28" x 37", 1995. Private Collection. 77

Boulevard des Capucines, Egg tempera on gesso panel, 16" x 12", 1990. Private collection. 62

Butterflies and Nun, Egg tempera on gesso panel, 20" x 28", 1992. Private collection. 67

Butterfly and Branch Shadows, Egg tempera on gesso panel, 18" x 14", 1980. Private collection, Naples, FL. 44

Chihuly Corridor, Egg tempera on gesso panel, 4" x 6", 2001. Collection of Myra Janco Daniels. Photo: Tim Stamm. 82, bottom

Claude's Nuns, Egg tempera on gesso panel, 20" x 24", 1990. Private collection. 63

Conversation, Oil on masonite, 26" x 46", circa 1955. Munson-Williams-Proctor Institute, Utica, NY. Photo: G. R. Farley. 17

Cool Corner, Egg tempera on gesso panel, 12 1/2" x 17 1/2", 1992. Private collection. 68

Cornered, Egg tempera on gesso panel, 9" x 12", 1997. Collection of Mr. & Mrs. John C. Wasmer, Jr. 80, bottom

Crossings, Egg tempera on gesso panel, 20" x 30", circa 1972. Private collection. 33

Curved Walls, Egg tempera on gesso panel, 19 1/2" x 13 1/2", 1982. Collection of Mr. & Mrs. Arthur Hurr. 47

Daughters Three, Egg tempera on gesso panel, 18" x 20", 2001-2. Private collection, Naples, FL. Photo: AP Alexander. 89

Eight by One, Egg tempera on gesso panel, approx. 15" x 26", circa 1988. Private collection in AZ. 54

Eleven Shadows, Egg tempera on gesso panel, 8" x 12", 1993. Private collection. 73

Fear, Egg tempera on gesso panel, 24" x 36", 1954. Collection of the Smithsonian American Art Museum, gift of Sara Roby Foundation. 14

Fright, egg tempera on gesso panel, 24" x 36", 1951. Private collection, Naples, FL. 6

Gaudi Perspectives, Egg tempera on gesso panel, 20" x 23 1/2", 2001. Private collection, Seattle, WA. Photo: Tim Stamm. 95

Ghosts, Egg tempera on gesso panel, 20" x 27", 1988. Private collection. 60

Gondolas and Balloons, Egg tempera on gesso panel, 12" x 16", 1991. Private collection. 66, bottom

Graffiti, Egg tempera on gesso panel, 24" x 36", 1980. Private collection, Naples, FL. 43

Key to the Universe, Egg tempera on gesso panel, 24" x 36", Joslyn Art Museum, Omaha, NE.
Inside Spread

La Jatte Aujourd 'hui, Egg tempera on gesso panel, 28" x 40", 1995. Private collection. Photo: Tim Stamm. 79

Labyrinth, Casein on panel, 32" x 48", 1951. Whitney Museum of American Art. Photo: Geoffrey Clements. 3

Lengthening Shadows, Egg tempera on gesso panel, approx. 9" x 13", circa 1973. Private collection. 38

Light Spangles, Egg tempera on gesso panel, 24" x 28", 2001. Private collection, Naples, FL. Photo: Tim Stamm. 84, top

Long Shadow, Egg tempera on gesso panel, 24" x 18", 1970. Private collection, Indianapolis, IN. 28

Madison Avenue Hawk, Oil on panel, 20" x 28", 1985. Private collection. 56

Midsummer Dreams, Egg tempera on gesso panel, 36" x 48", 1984-5. Private collection. 53

Morning Light, Acrylic on paperboard, 28" x 37", 1995. Collection of Florence O'Donnell Wasmer Gallery, Ursuline College. Photo: Robert Wetzler. x

Morpho Aega, Acrylic on paperboard, 39 1/4" x 28 1/2", 1980. Private collection, Tuscaloosa, AL. 45

Museum Corridor, Acrylic on paperboard, 24" x 36", 1974. Private collection. 39

Nine Angels, Egg tempera on gesso panel, 18" x 24", 2001-2. Private collection, Naples, FL. Photo: Tim Stamm. 88

Number 54, Egg tempera on gesso panel, 24" x 36", 1970. Private collection, Naples, FL. 27

Nun and Bicycle, Egg tempera on gesso panel, 8" x 10", 1976. Private collection. 41

Nun and Posters, Egg tempera on gesso panel, 14" x 28", circa 1953. Private collection. 10